LET'S PLAY TENNIS!

A Guide for Parents and Kids

by Andy Ace

Written and Illustrated by Patricia Egart

ISBN: 978-0-9819860-3-6
Library of Congress Catalog Number: 2009941192
Printed in the United States of America
First Printing:
14 13 12 11 10 5 4 3 2 1

Edited by Kellie M. Hultgren
Layout by Chris Fayers
Art editing by Kara C. Johnson

1935 Berkshire Drive
Eagan, Minnesota 55122
651.452.0463
www.AmberSkyePublishing.com

ENDORSED BY
NORTHERN
www.northern.usta.com

To order, visit www.ItascaBooks.com or www.AndyAceTennis.com
or call 1-800-901-3480. Reseller discounts available.

Andy Ace takes parents and kids on a fun-filled journey from the sporting goods department, to the courts to learn the strokes and tips for practicing, and ends with an exciting match with Danny Deuce! Full-color illustrations are included with easy to follow descriptions to help players of all ages get out on the courts and learn to play tennis.

Tales of the Tennis Tigers Series
Let's Play Tennis! A Guide for Parents and Kids
Coming soon:
Alley Learns Something New
Andy and the Two Racquets
Andy and Fair Play

Dear Parents and Future Tennis Stars,

I wrote this book to help my mom and dad, my sister Alley, and her friends Chip and Lucy to get out on the courts and play tennis. In it, you will learn about the game of tennis, including things like:

- what equipment you will need
- how to make the court smaller for beginners
- how to hold the racquet
- how to warm up
- how to move your feet
- how to serve and hit all the strokes

Dad **Mom**

Chip **Alley**

Lucy

I have included my favorite games and drills which parents and kids can do together. You will learn about tennis etiquette and sportsmanship.

Danny

You also will learn about match play as you follow me through an exciting match with Danny Deuce.

Note to Parents: Tennis is a great family sport! This guide is intended to help you learn to play tennis, too! You will be able to beat your kid at first. You will let them win sometimes, of course. At some point, they will start beating you for real. Good luck in dealing with that!

Note to Kids: Your goal is to beat your parents by the time you are twelve years old. Your parents will spend the rest of their lives trying to beat you. Don't ever let them win. They will know!

I am twelve years old, and I have been playing tennis since I was five. Did I mention that playing tennis is a blast? I play on a team with my friends, and I play almost every day.

Now, let's get started!
Your friend,

Andy Ace

About the Game of Tennis

Tennis is a game played on a rectangular court with a net in the middle. The object of the game is to hit the ball over the net and into the opposite court within the boundaries. Players need to hit the ball back over the net after only one bounce or before the ball bounces.

Singles is a tennis match played between two players. **Doubles** is a match played by four players as two doubles teams. Boys and girls can play doubles together for **mixed doubles** matches. Most tennis is played on **hard** courts, but it is also played on courts made of **clay** or **grass**.

Tennis can be played by people of all ages. There are tournaments and leagues for ages eight to ninety. Tennis can be played by people in wheelchairs, too.

Tennis is a lifetime sport!

Stuff You Need

Let's start out at the tennis department of your favorite store. One of the great things about tennis is that you don't need a lot of expensive equipment. The basics are:

Racquet It is important to buy a racquet that is the right length for your age. If you are tall for your age, you may want to buy a longer racquet. Here are general guidelines:

Ages 3 & 4	19"
Ages 5 & 6	21"
Ages 7 & 8	23 "
Ages 9 & 10	25"
Ages 11 to Adult	26–27½"

**Ages 8 &
Under
Red &
Yellow
Felt Ball**

**Ages 10 &
Under
Orange
& Yellow
Felt Ball**

**Ages 11 +
Yellow
Felt Ball**

Balls For ages three to eight, the oversized, red-and-yellow, low-compression felt balls work best. For ages nine and ten, the orange-and-yellow, low-compression felt balls work best. These balls bounce lower and move more slowly, so the player develops the proper strokes with more success.

Ball Hopper Don't head to the courts with just one can of balls. Buy a hopper and fill it up. You can spend more time hitting and serving without stopping to pick up balls.

My dog, Topspin, loves my hopper!

Tennis Shoe

Shoes All athletic shoes used to be called tennis shoes, and everyone used tennis shoes for every sport. Now there are shoes made specifically for each sport to prevent injury, to improve performance, and to match the playing surface. It's important to wear tennis shoes to play tennis. You can see that tennis shoes have a rounded edge on the sole. There's a ton of side-to-side movement in tennis, so a cross-trainer or running shoe could cause you to hurt your ankle or knee. Also, tennis shoes do not mark up tennis courts.

Running Shoe

Socks Wear sports socks with extra padding in the toe and heel.

Clothing Players should wear clothing that allows them to have a second tennis ball on them when they are serving.

Boys can wear shorts or pants with pockets. **Girls** can wear shorts or pants with pockets or tennis skirts with built-in tennis underwear.

This is important for matches and for practices. Many practice drills require players to have extra balls in their pockets. That way, players can perform drills without stopping to pick up balls.

Water Bottle Buy a large, insulated water bottle and write your name on it. Bring it with you every time you play tennis and take frequent drinks. Don't bring a dinky little water bottle out there. It won't be enough if it gets hot or if you have a long match. It's not fun to wait at a match or practice for a player who needs to leave the courts to keep refilling a water bottle.

Andy Ace

Parts of the Court

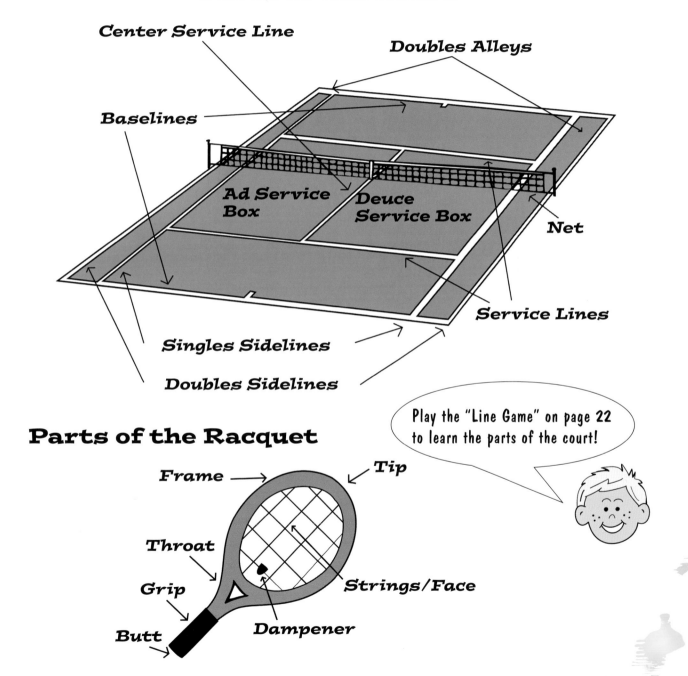

Center Service Line

Doubles Alleys

Baselines

Ad Service Box

Deuce Service Box

Net

Service Lines

Singles Sidelines

Doubles Sidelines

Parts of the Racquet

Frame →

Tip

Throat

Grip

Strings/Face

Butt

Dampener

Play the "Line Game" on page 22 to learn the parts of the court!

QuickStart Courts and Scoring

Players under the age of eleven should not start playing on a full size court. That would be like putting a T-ball team on a professional baseball field. QuickStart modifies the court sizes and equipment to help kids ages ten and younger play tennis. The younger age groups use modified scoring that is easy to understand and shortens up the length of matches.

Court Sizes for Ages 8 & Under

This age group plays on a 36-foot-deep by 18-foot-wide court. Set up mini-nets, using the doubles sidelines to form the baselines. If mini-nets are not available, use the service lines as the baseline boundaries, and use the center service lines and the doubles sidelines for the side boundaries.

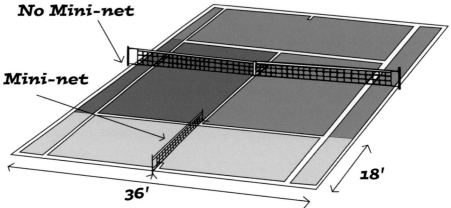

No Mini-net

Mini-net

18'

36'

Scoring for Ages 8 & Under

There are seven points in a game. The first player to score seven points wins the game. The first player to win two games wins the match. Players may use an underhand serve and hit the ball out of their hand. Players serve two points in a row, then switch servers. As players advance to competition, they will use the same scoring used for a set tiebreak (explained on page 28).

 Use the red-and-yellow, low-compression balls and the right length racquet for the age of the child.

Court Sizes for Ages 10 & Under

This age group plays on a 60-foot-deep by 27-foot-wide court. Use the singles sidelines for the doubles sidelines and use sidewalk chalk to mark the baselines 9 feet in from the regulation baselines. Mark singles sidelines 3 feet in from the regulation singles sidelines.

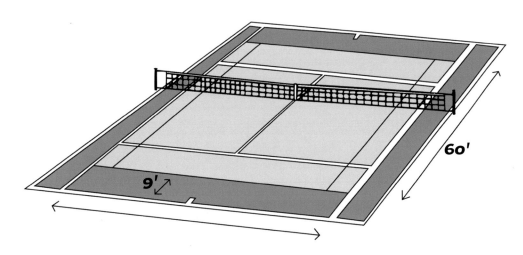

Scoring for Ages 10 & Under

This age group plays the best of two out of three short sets using regulation scoring (explained on page 25). The first to win four games wins a set. For the third set, play a set tiebreak (explained on page 28). Players may serve with an overhand motion or an underhand motion.

Use the orange-and-yellow, low-compression balls and the right length racquet.

Warming Up the Right Way

You need to warm up properly before you play tennis. The best way to warm up is to take a slow jog around your tennis courts and then stretch your muscles by moving them. Here are a few of my favorite ways to stretch:

Crazy Run Jog across the court and back while circling your arms and trying to kick your butt with your heels.

Toe and Heel Walks Walk on your toes across the court and back. Then walk on your heels across and back.

Monster Walks Walk across the court, taking huge steps and bending your knees to get low to the court. Hold your arms out at your sides for balance.

Robot Walks Hold your arms out in front and kick your legs up one at a time, trying to touch your hands with your toes.

Butt Kicks Walk across the court while trying to kick your butt with alternating heels.

Arm Circles Circle your arms forwards and backwards.

Are you warmed up and ready to play tennis?

How to Move Your Feet

It is important to move your feet a lot when you play tennis so you can be ready to hit a great shot!

Ready Position In the ready position, face the net, hold your racquet in front, bend your knees, and keep your feet moving. Stay on the balls of your feet—don't settle back on your heels. Start in the ready position before you hit the ball, and go back to the ready position after you hit the ball.

Keep your feet moving!

Split Step "Split step" by bouncing on the balls of your feet as your opponent hits the ball, so you can move quickly in any direction.

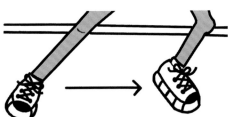

Shuffle "Shuffle" to move sideways so you can face your opponent and be ready to hit the next shot.

Set-up Steps When you are running to hit a ball, use long steps to get there quickly. As you get close to the ball and are about to hit it, use small "set-up steps" so you are balanced when you make contact.

Play "Ball-Race" on page 22 to practice set-up steps!

Hit Off Your Front Foot Beginners should transfer their weight to their front foot as they hit the ball to stay balanced.

How to Serve

The serve starts every point. Use the Continental Grip for the serve.

The Continental Grip *To find this grip, place the V formed by the thumb and index finger of your dominant hand on the edge of the frame and slide it down to the grip. Then wrap your thumb and fingers around the grip.*

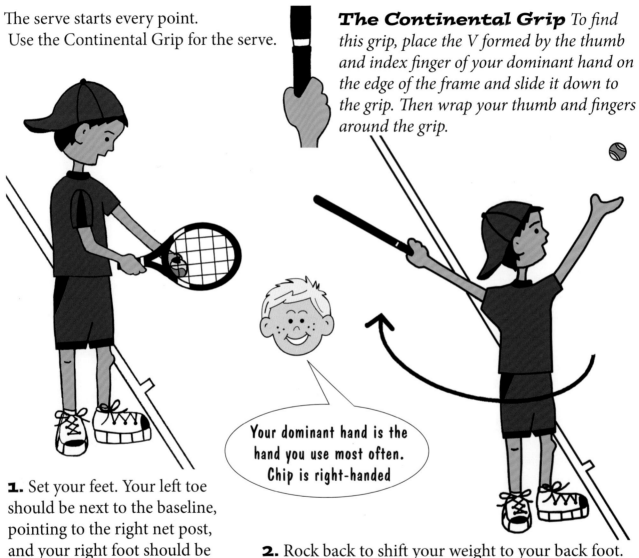

Your dominant hand is the hand you use most often. Chip is right-handed

1. Set your feet. Your left toe should be next to the baseline, pointing to the right net post, and your right foot should be parallel to the baseline. Your weight should be on your front foot. Hold the ball next to the strings.

2. Rock back to shift your weight to your back foot. As you rock back, your left arm should push the ball up for the toss. Your racquet arm should swing up so you make the letter Y with your body. The knuckles of your right hand should be up.

4. Swing up at the ball and meet it above and slightly in front of your head, with your hitting arm fully extended. Your left arm will naturally drop as you swing at the ball. Follow through across your body.

Take your hopper to the courts and practice your serve often.

3. Drop your racquet behind your back. Leave the tossing arm up after the toss.

Note: Some players may prefer to start serving with the Eastern Forehand Grip explained on page 14. This is fine but encourage them to move to the Continental Grip as they advance.

How to Hit a Forehand Groundstroke

A forehand is a one-handed stroke used to hit a ball after it has bounced on the court on your dominant side. Use the Eastern Forehand Grip.

The Eastern Forehand Grip *To find this grip, place the palm of your dominant hand on the strings, then slide it down to the grip. Then wrap your thumb and fingers around the grip.*

Alley is right-handed just like Chip.

1. Start in the ready position with your racquet out in front.

2. Turn sideways, taking your non-dominant hand off of the grip. Leave that hand out in front for balance. Bring your racquet back and drop the racquet in a circling motion to about knee height.

Swing low to high!

3. Turn your hips and bring the racquet forward to meet the ball to the side and out in front of your body. Shift your weight to your front foot as you hit the ball.

4. Follow through upwards and across your body. Catch the racquet on the follow-through with your non-dominant hand. End with your racquet over your non-dominant shoulder.

How to Hit a Two-Handed Backhand Groundstroke

A backhand is a stroke that you use to hit a ball after it has bounced on the court on your non-dominant side. Use the Two-Handed Backhand Grip.

The Two-Handed Backhand Grip
While holding the racquet with the Continental Grip, place the palm of the other hand on the strings and slide your hand down. Place it right next to the other hand so your hands are touching.

1. Start in the ready position with your racquet out in front.

2. Turn and bring the racquet back with both hands, making a small circling motion and dropping the racquet to about knee height.

Swing low to high! Follow through with both hands on the racquet.

3. Turn your hips and bring the racquet forward to meet the ball to the side and out in front of your body. Shift your weight to your front foot as you hit the ball.

4. Follow through upwards and across your body, keeping both hands on the racquet to finish.

How to Lob

The lob is used to hit the ball over a player who is close to the net. It is also used to give yourself more time to recover after running to hit a wide shot. Use the Eastern Forehand or Two-Handed Backhand Grip for lobbing.

Learn to lob and use it often!

1. Use your forehand or backhand groundstroke to hit a lob. Angle the strings towards the sky when you hit the ball.

2. Follow through high after you make contact with the ball.

How to Hit an Overhead

The overhead is used to return a lob. Use the Continental Grip for overheads.

1. When you see a high ball coming, turn sideways to your right, drop your racquet behind your back, point up at the ball with your left arm and move your feet to get under the ball.

2. Swing your racquet up to meet the ball above your head and slightly out in front. Your left arm will naturally drop as you swing at the ball. Follow through across your body.

How to Hit a Forehand Volley

The forehand volley is a shot used to hit a ball out of the air before it bounces on your dominant side. Use the Continental Grip for volleys.

Lucy is right-handed.

1. From the ready position at the net with your racquet high, use your right shoulder to pull the racquet back as if you were going to high-five the ball.

2. Use a short swing to meet the ball out in front of your body, stepping into the shot with your left foot.

How to Hit a Backhand Volley

The backhand volley is a shot used to hit a ball out of the air before it bounces on your non-dominant side. Use your backhand volley for balls hit right at your body.

1. From the ready position at net with your racquet high, turn to your left and pull the racquet back as if you were going to high-five the ball with the other side of the racquet.

2. Use a short swing to meet the ball out in front of your body, stepping into the shot with your right foot.

Andy's Favorite Games and Drills

Here are a few of my favorite games and drills. Parents and kids can use them to learn and practice tennis together. Remember, use the recommended balls and do the activities on a court that is the right size for the age of the child.

When learning the groundstrokes, parents should explain and demonstrate the stroke as in the diagrams. Show your child how the ball is hit from the side of the body. Have them copy you as you do the stroke a few times. Then "feed" some balls to them by gently tossing with an underhand motion or by hitting with your racquet. Feed from a few feet away at first. Then gradually move away as their shots succeed. Then start alternating feeds to their left side, to their right side, in front, and close to them, so they learn to move sideways and up and back. Remind them to swing low to high.

Ball Race This is a fun footwork game. Each player sets their racquet on the deuce court doubles sideline and places three balls on the ad court doubles sideline. Players start by their racquets. On "Go," both players run to retrieve one ball at a time and place them on their racquet. The first player with all three balls on their racquet wins. I play, too, setting four balls for me on the doubles sideline to make this a fair game.

The Line Game This fun warm-up teaches players the areas of the court. I ask Alley and Chip, "Who wants to be the last one to the baseline?" and we all race to be the first to the baseline. Then I change it to "to the net, to the ad singles sideline, to the deuce doubles sideline," and so on.

In any drill, have beginning players say "Bounce-hit" every time they hit the ball. They say "Bounce" when the ball hits the ground, so they know they should have their racquet circling back. They say "Hit" as they hit the ball. This helps with timing, so they can develop consistency. Don't start any game or drill until players are moving their feet!

Bounce-Hit!

Jacks Alley and I play this to practice rallying the ball. We try to get three hits in a row each with one ball, counting out loud every time we hit the ball over the net. If one of us misses, we both go back to zero. We both start a few feet from the net and use very short swings. Then, after we reach our goal of three in a row, we take one step back and repeat until we are both at the baselines. We use longer swings as we move back to the baselines.

Four Ball Game Alley starts at the baseline, and I feed a deep ball to her forehand. If she gets that in, I feed a short ball to her forehand. If she gets that in, I feed her a high ball to volley. If she gets that in, I feed her a lob for an overhead. If she makes that, she gets a "big point." If she misses any shot, she gets a second chance. If she misses the second ball, she starts over at the baseline. When Chip and Lucy are there, they get a turn when she misses twice at one shot. Alley, Chip and Lucy try to be the first to five big points. Play the same game and feed balls to the backhand side.

Four Ball Game II This is similar to the previous game. Alley will play out each point against Chip, Lucy or me. If she wins the first point from the baseline, she gets a short ball, then a volley, then an overhead. If she loses any point, she gets a second chance. If she loses that point, she starts over at the baseline. Alley needs to win all four points to get one big point. We play until Alley gets five points. Then the players switch ends of the court, or we play the same game and I feed balls to the player's backhand.

Scoring Game This is a good game to practice serving and to learn how to keep score (explained on page 25). Alley plays a game against an imaginary opponent. She serves a ball to the deuce service box. If she gets it in with one or two tries, she gets a point and calls it "15." Then she serves to the ad service box. She says the score before each serve. She continues to serve until she has a game: "15, 30, 40, Game." If she does not get the serve in with two tries, her imaginary opponent wins the point. We play until Alley wins four games.

Driveway Tennis When Alley and I can't make it to the courts, we play driveway tennis. We set up a court in our driveway using a mini-net or a rope tied to two chairs. We use the driveway width for sidelines and use masking tape or sidewalk chalk to mark two baselines about eighteen feet from the net. We play games to seven points, taking turns every two points to start the point with an underhand feed, or we play games to twenty-one points, switching servers every five points as in ping-pong.

T-ball Tennis This is a modified version of a regular tennis game. I played this with Alley when she was learning to serve and couldn't always get the ball in with two tries. If she missed both serves, I fed the ball to her to start the point. This is just like T-ball, where players never strike out.

When I see that Alley is getting tired, we pick up the balls and go and get ice cream cones!

The Big Match

Danny Deuce and I are going to play a match. A match consists of the best of two out of three sets. A set consists of six games. The first player to win six games by a margin of two games wins the set. If we each win a set, we will play a match tiebreak.

Before the match, Danny and I met at the net for the spin.

The Spin *One player spins and the other player calls "Up" or "Down," predicting how the emblem on the butt of the racquet will be positioned after the spin. The winner of the spin can choose to serve, to receive, or the side they want to start on, or they may give the choice to their opponent. The other player gets a choice of side if the winner of the spin chooses to serve or receive. If the winner of the spin chooses the side, the other player may choose to serve or to receive.*

Danny won the spin and chose to serve. I chose the side with my back to the wind.

Next, Danny and I hit the ball back and forth over the net to warm up.

The Rally Warm-Up *"Rally" means to hit the ball back and forth. Both players should start at the service lines and rally from a short distance. Gradually move back to the baselines and rally from there. Then bring one player to the net to hit volleys and overheads. Switch and bring the other player to the net to volley and hit overheads. Finally, players take turns warming up their serves.*

Don't try to win the warm-up. Make sure you are hitting the ball to your opponent while warming up. Save your shots to the open court for your match.

Our family and friends were at the big match!

About Cheering *A lot of people think you have to be quiet as a mouse during a tennis match. This is not true. We always cheer for our teammates at matches. The key is to know when to cheer. Cheer when someone makes a great shot. Don't cheer when someone misses.*

Danny said the score, "Zero-Zero, Love-Love," then served to start the match.

What the Server Does *The server must say the game score before serving each point. The server always says their own score first. The server should also say the set score before the first serve of each game.*

The first point is always served from the deuce side to the cross-court service box. The server gets two chances to serve the ball in. If both serves are missed, it is a double fault and the point goes to the receiver. The second point is served from the ad side to the cross-court service box and continues to alternate to each side until the game ends. A point is won when one player does not get the ball over the net and into the opponent's court, or when it bounces twice.

Scoring *Each game starts at Love–Love. "Love" means "zero" in tennis.*

The first point is called "15."   The second point is called "30."

The third point is called "40."   The fourth point is called "Game."

You must win a game by a margin of two points.

Danny won the first three points. I won the next three points, so our first game was tied with the score of 40–40. At 40–40, the score is called "Deuce."

Danny won the next point. The point after deuce is called "Advantage:" "Ad-in" if the server won the previous point or "Ad-out" if the receiver won the point.

The point after an advantage will either be "Game" or will go back to "Deuce."

Danny won the point after "Ad-in," so he won the game.

After the first game, we changed ends of the court.

The Changeover *Switch ends of the court after every odd game. So you switch after one game, three games, five games, and so on. Use your time on the changeover to take a drink of water and to think about your match.*

Match Strategy *My best advice to beginning players is to always try to get the ball back over the net one more time than your opponent does. Learn to be consistent. Keep a positive attitude and never give up. There is no time limit in tennis. Even if you are behind by a big margin, you can always come back. I always try to get to every ball and win as many points and games as I can. Try your hardest and always have fun!*

I had a feeling this was going to be a long and close match. Danny and I are both very consistent players who work hard to get every ball back.

I started serving the next game. Right after I served, a player walked behind our court to get to the next court during our point. We had to start the point over again.

Be Considerate *Always wait until a point has ended to get to another court or to get your ball.*

I started the point over and won three points in a row, so the score was 40–Love.

Danny hit a shot that landed very close to the baseline.

I wasn't sure if the ball was in or out, so I called Danny's ball in.

Now the score was 40–15.

Danny returned my serve, and it landed right behind the baseline.

Danny's ball was clearly out, so I said "Out" and I used the hand signal. I won the point and the game.

Line Calls *Players call the lines on their own side of the court. Make calls quickly, but make sure the ball bounces before you make a call. If you are not sure, call the ball in.*

In *A ball is in if it lands inside the boundary line or on the line. You don't need to make an in call very often because you will play balls that are in. In some cases, your opponent will not be sure if a ball was in or out after the point has ended. Say "In" and hold your palm down for the hand signal.*

Out *If a ball bounces outside the boundary line and doesn't touch the line, say "Out" and use the hand signal with your index finger pointing up.*

I won the first set with the score of six games to four games. I used the black scorecards and Danny used red.

In the second set, Danny and I were tied at six games, so we played a set tiebreak.

Scoring the Set Tiebreak

A set tiebreak is played until someone wins seven points by a margin of two.

The player whose turn it is to serve will start the tiebreak, serving one point to the deuce court.

The other player then serves the next two points, starting to the ad court.

Each player then serves alternately for two consecutive points, always starting to the ad court.

Players change ends of the court every six points and at the conclusion of the tiebreak.

The player who first wins seven points by at least a margin of two wins the tiebreak and the set.

The player who started the tiebreak as the server will start as the receiver for the next set.

Scoring the Match Tiebreak

A match tiebreak to ten points is often used in place of a full third set in match play. The procedure is the same as the set tiebreak, except the first player to win ten points by at least a margin of two wins the match.

Danny won the set tiebreak, so he won the second set with the score of seven games to six games.

Now we needed to play a match tiebreak to ten points to decide the match winner!

On the first point of the tiebreak, I hit a shot to the open court that I was sure Danny couldn't reach. He got to the ball and hit a great shot back and won the point. I clapped my hand on my strings to let him know I thought he made a great shot.

Hand to Racquet Sign _Let your opponent know that you think it's really cool when they make a great shot. The universal sign is to raise your racquet up and clap your hand on the strings._

The score stayed close throughout the tiebreak!

Finally, I was serving with the score at 9-8.

I hit a great serve to Danny's backhand. He hit a weak shot back over the net which landed near the service line. I raced to the service line and hit the ball to Danny's forehand. Danny tried to lob the ball over me. I hit an overhead. I moved to the net and hit the next ball with a volley to win the point!

Danny and I shook hands after our close match!

Shake Hands after the Match
After the match, go directly to the net to shake hands with your opponent. Say "Nice match!" Shake your opponent's hand even if you are upset about the outcome.

Now, you need to figure out what the final match score was. Hint: the winner's score is always listed first. See the next page for the answer!

The final score was 6-4, 6-7, 1-0

I won the first set with the score of six games to four games. I lost the second set with the score of six games to seven games. When a tiebreak is used in place of a full third set, the score is reported 1–0.

Now, get going and hit the tennis courts! Here is some more information to help you:

Programs and Tournaments

Try to find a program in your community or at a club that offers the QuickStart format along with a team program such as USTA Jr. Team Tennis. My friends and I play on a team, the Tennis Tigers, and we have a lot of fun. If you cannot find a program, ask your parents to start one.

As soon as you are ready, enter tournaments and play in both singles and doubles events. Check with your community and clubs to see if they offer junior tournaments. Be sure to start at the beginner level.

Helpful Web Sites

www.usta.com

This is the Web site of the United States Tennis Association (USTA). There are seventeen USTA sections in the United States. Click on your section and you will find many resources to help you find a tennis program near you, find someone to play with, tournaments, find a public or private facility, and much more.

www.quickstarttennis.com

Here you can find more information on QuickStart Tennis and places to buy low-compression balls, racquets, and mini-nets.

Things to Do!

Kid's Checklist	Parent's Checklist
✓ Set a date with your parent to start playing tennis.	✓ Buy racquets and balls for you and your child.
✓ Set up a court in your driveway and play driveway tennis.	✓ Locate tennis courts near your house.
✓ Invite a friend to play tennis with you.	✓ Invite a friend to play tennis with you.
✓ Hold a driveway tennis tournament for your friends and neighbors.	✓ Invite the families in your neighborhood to join you at the courts.
✓ Join a tennis team.	✓ Help your child find a team program and tournaments to participate in.
✓ Play in a tournament.	✓ Check out the tennis programs at your child's school.
✓ Watch the pros play tennis on TV.	✓ Take your child to see a local high school or college match.
✓ Beat your mom or dad at tennis!	✓ Join a tennis team.

Additional Tips for Mom and Dad

Remember the 5-1 Rule: For every corrective comment you make to your child, make five positive comments!

Keep play sessions short for young kids; forty-five minutes maximum for ages eight and under; sixty minutes maximum for ages ten and under.

Change games and drills often. Change a game before it gets "old".

Have fun!

My Tennis Journal

My name: _Dominique_

Date I first played tennis: _____

Name of my first tennis coach: _____

Date of my first match: _____ Opponent:_____ Score:_____

My first team name: _____

My first tournament: _____

Date of my first big win over Mom/Dad: _____

My best shot: _____

My favorite strategy: _____

My favorite professional tennis player: _____